BREAKDANCE
Coloring & Activity Book
by Idan Boaz

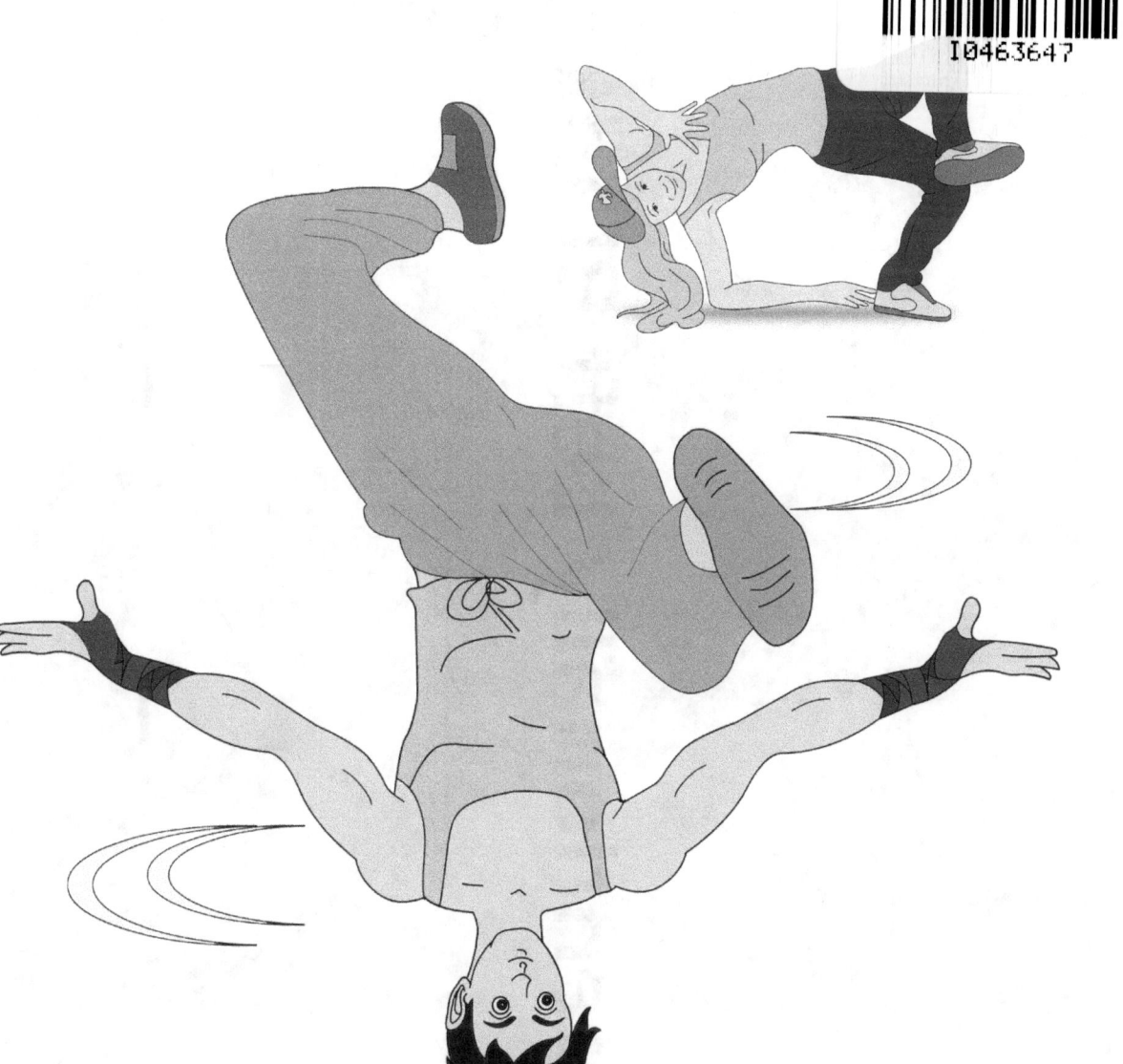

ISBN-13: 978-1544091259

ISBN-10: 1544091257

ILLUSTRATION BY
ATONDRILLA PRODUCTION

Intentionally Left Blank

This book Belongs to

_____

_____

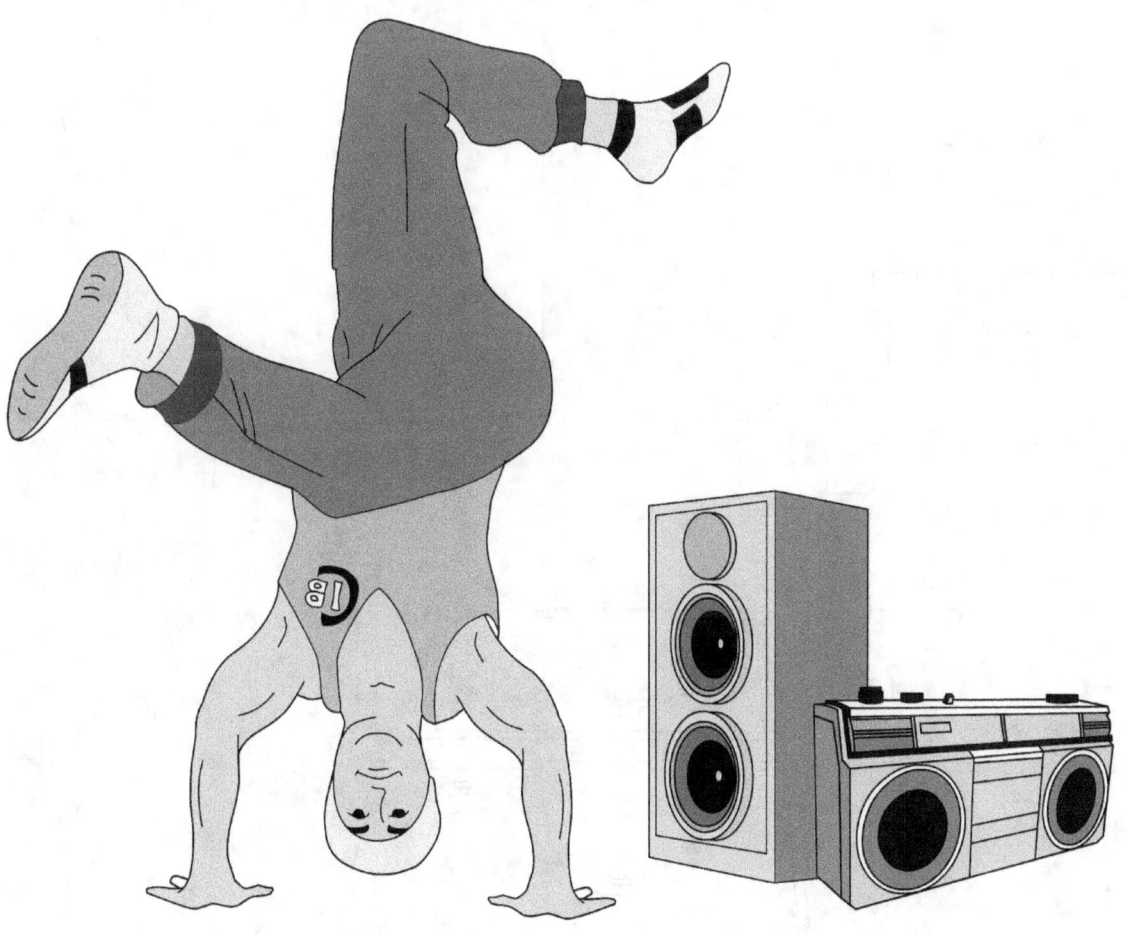

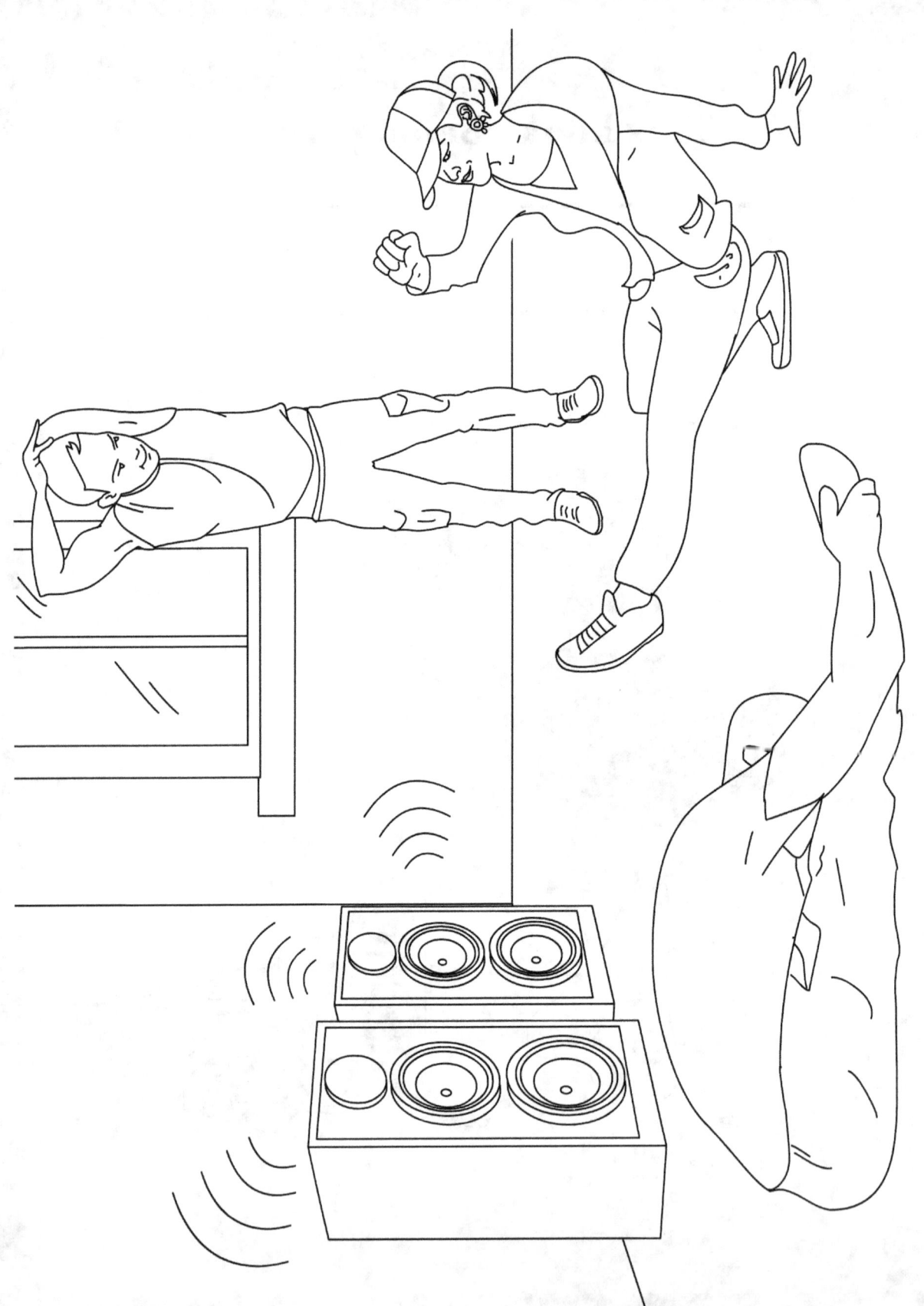

Welcome to the school of breakdancing. we are about to show you what we are made of, get yourself ready as we finished stretching our body.

This move is the two-step, they move their two feet in time with the beat, before they pull out the next move in their breakdancing groove.

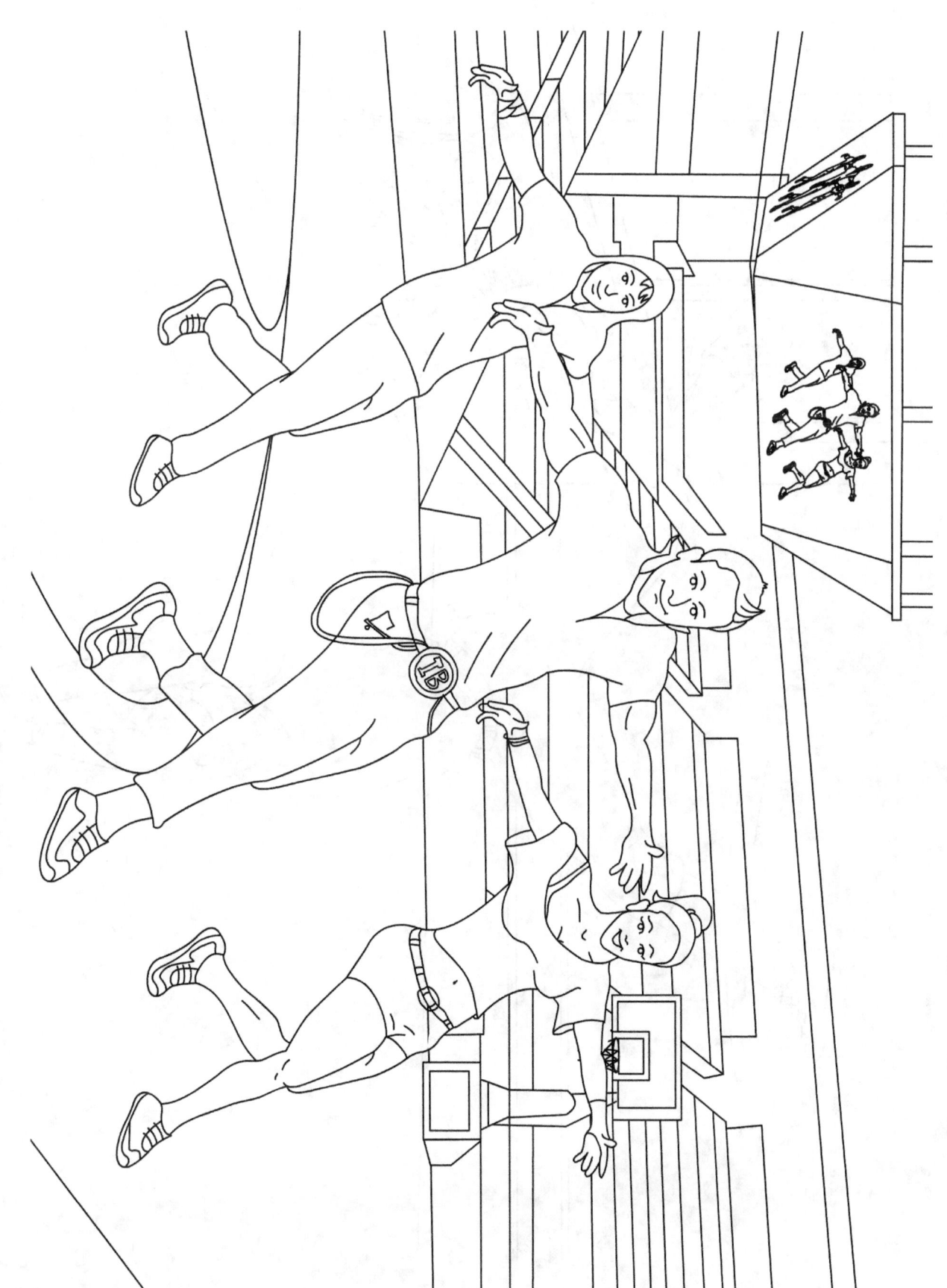

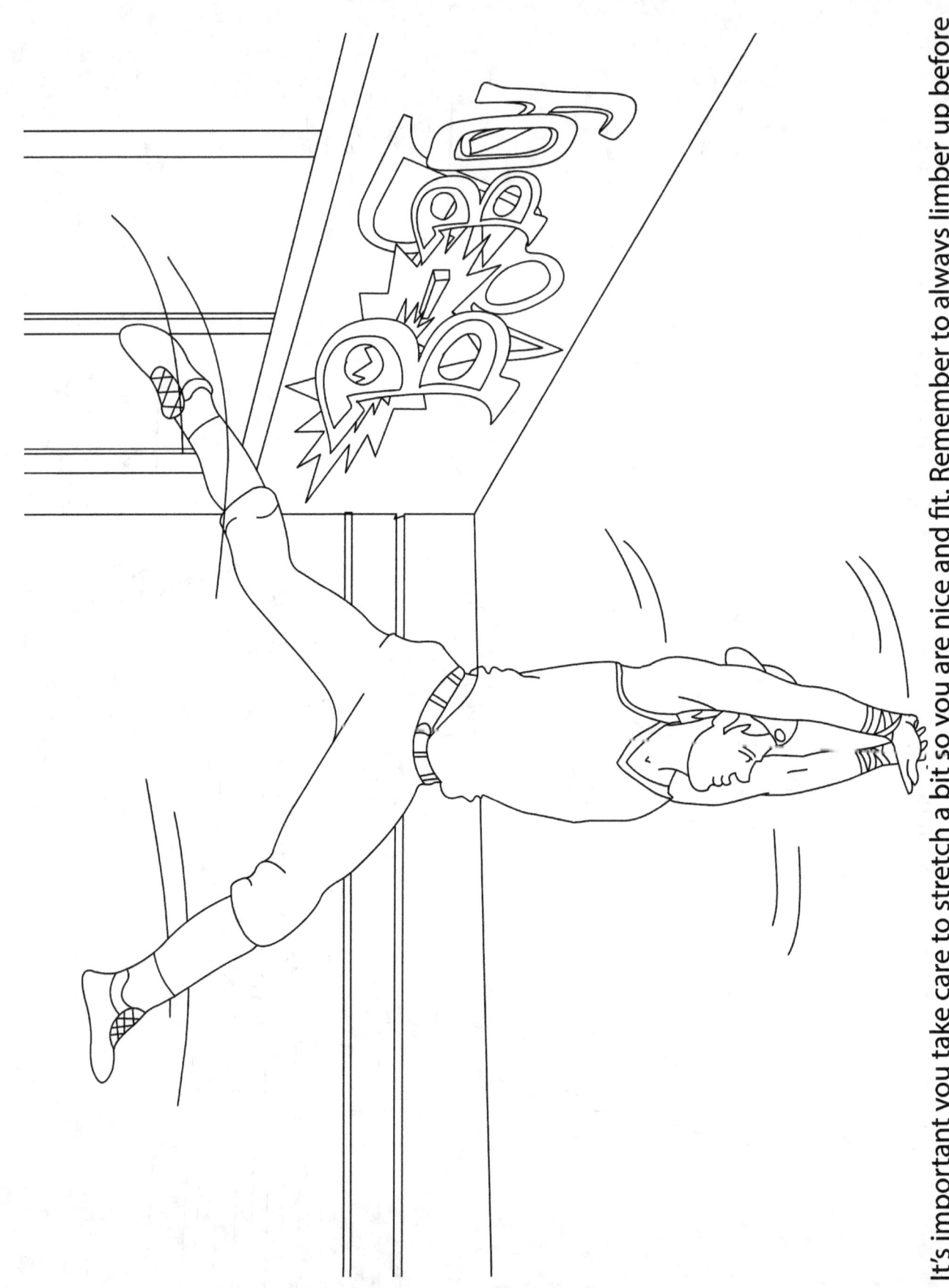

It's important you take care to stretch a bit so you are nice and fit. Remember to always limber up before you let your super moves erupt.

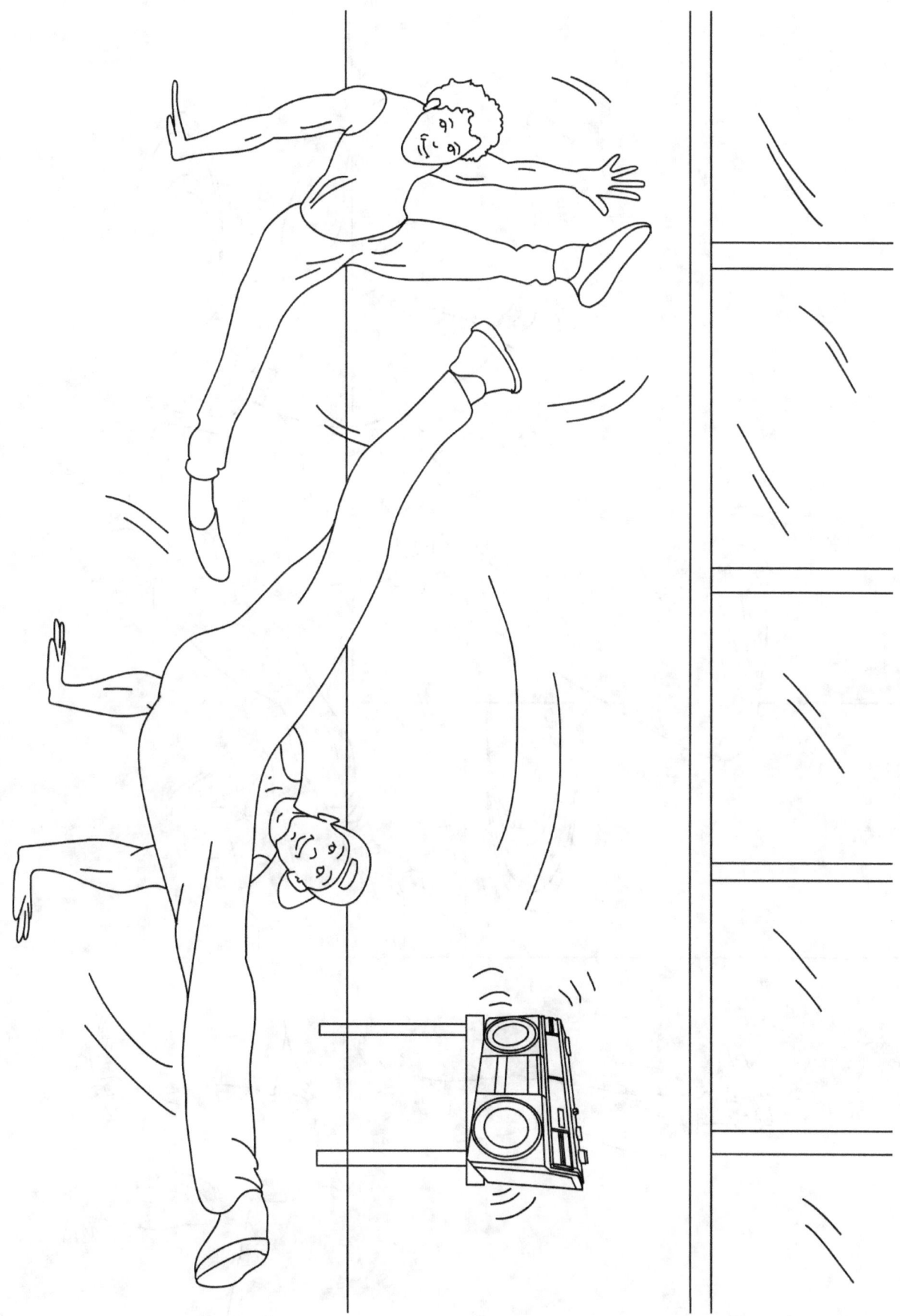

This move is advanced and called Flare. A power move for the experienced and ones who dare. The legs are swung in a windmill and its execution takes enormous skill.

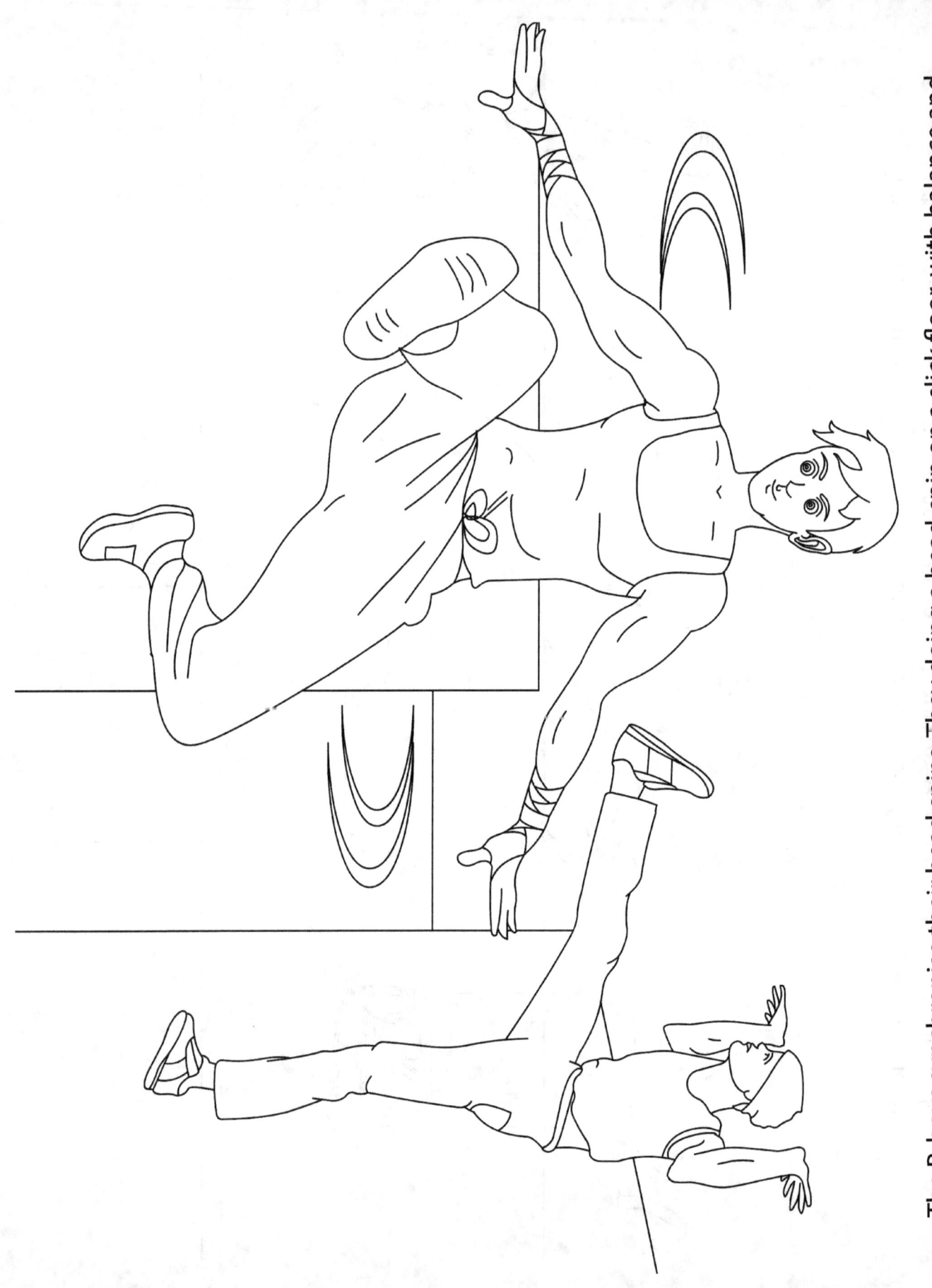

The B-boys synchronise their head spins. They doing a head-spin on a slick floor, with balance and strength so they spins more. they're like a spinning-top on a table, twisting like magic in a fable.

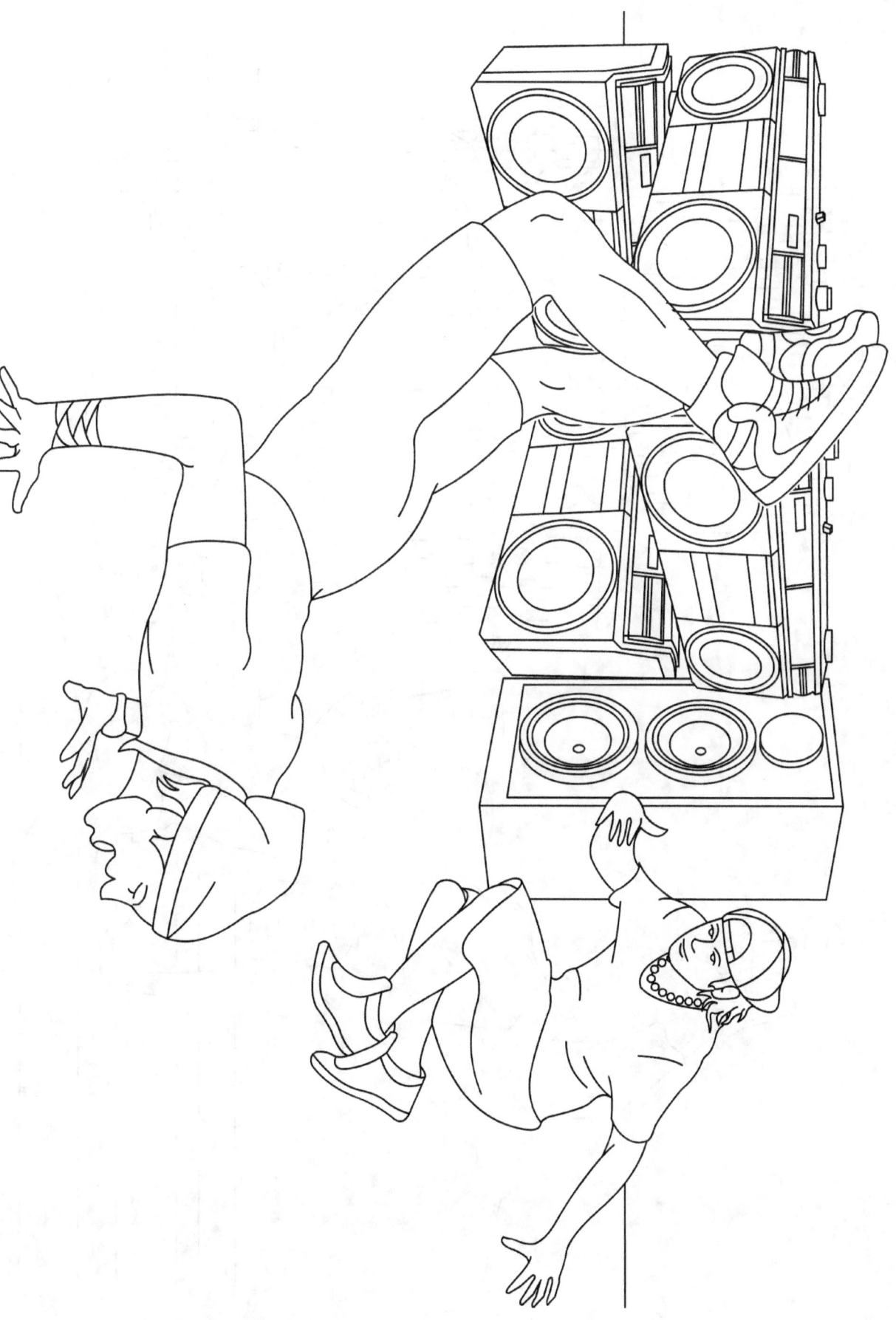

Witness the worm, a move sure to make heads turn, a wiggle up and down, like a smile changed into a frown. Pull this one out at a party for all the laughs to be hearty.

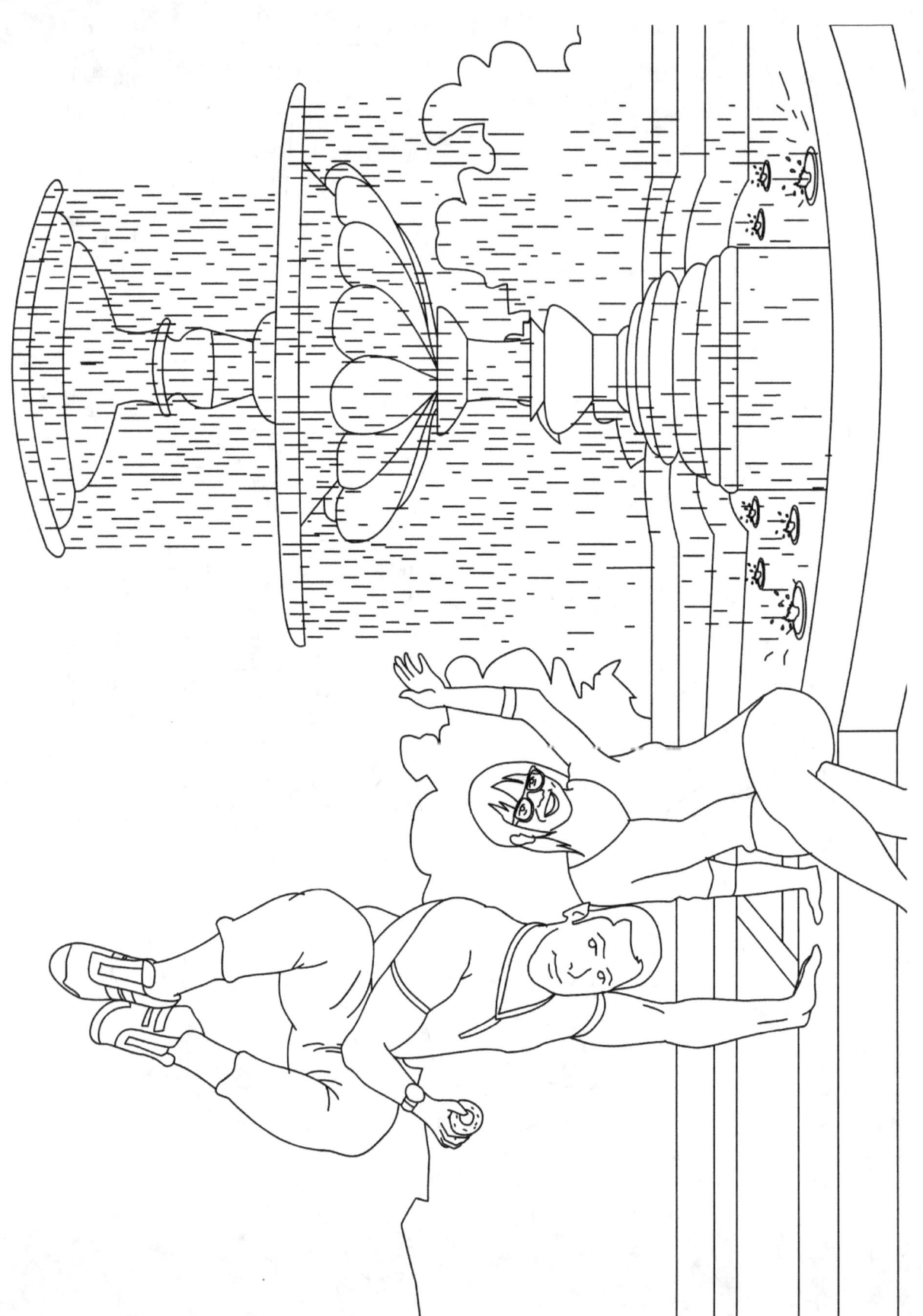

A simple freeze move which needs the flexibility to be done with ease. A freeze is where you maintain a difficult position for a few seconds before the next move beckons. For flexibility, practice touching your toe and see how far you can go.

These B-boys and B-girls make up a breakdancing crew. They take it in turns to show all they have learned, performing their best techniques to put you on the edge of your seat.

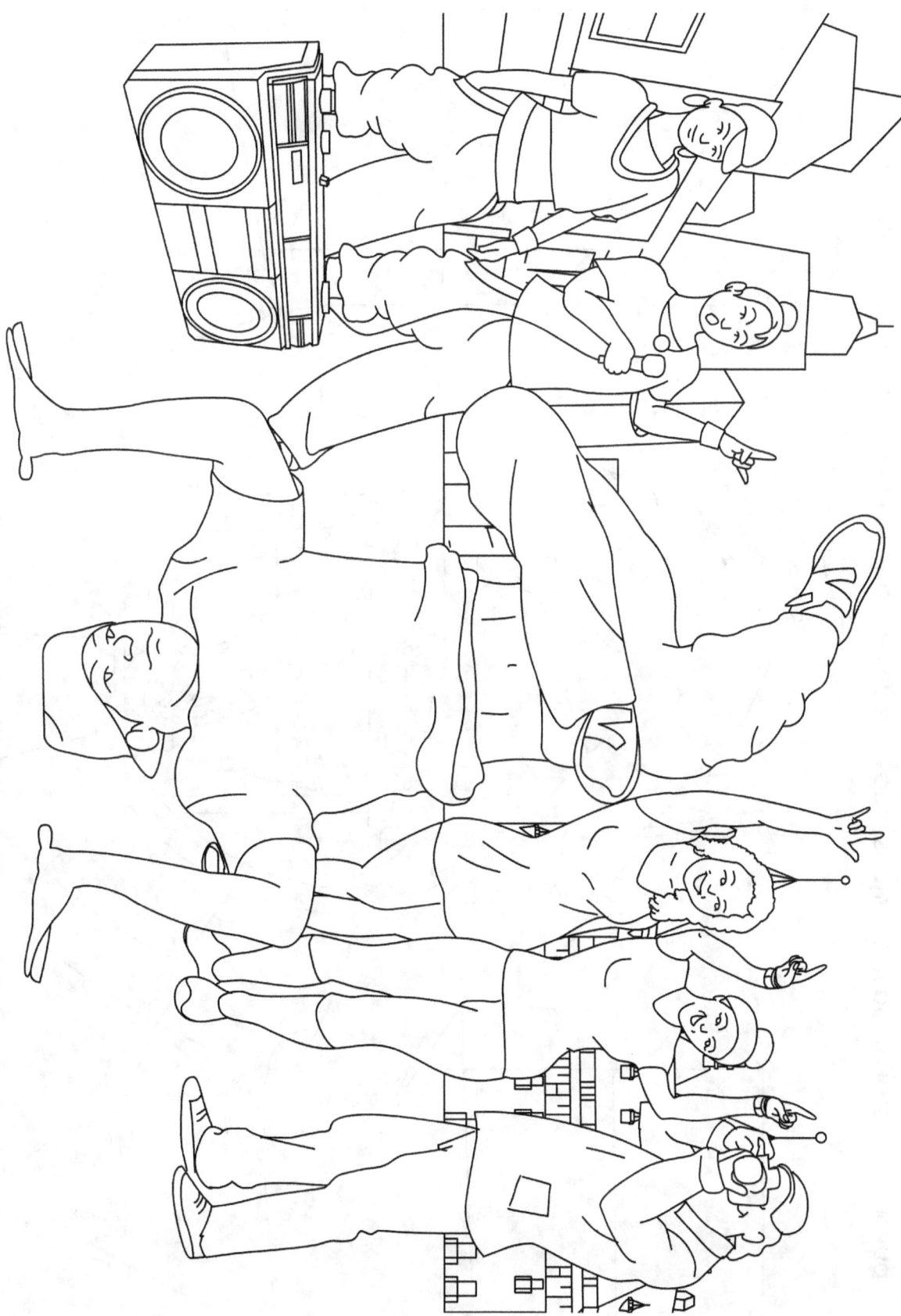

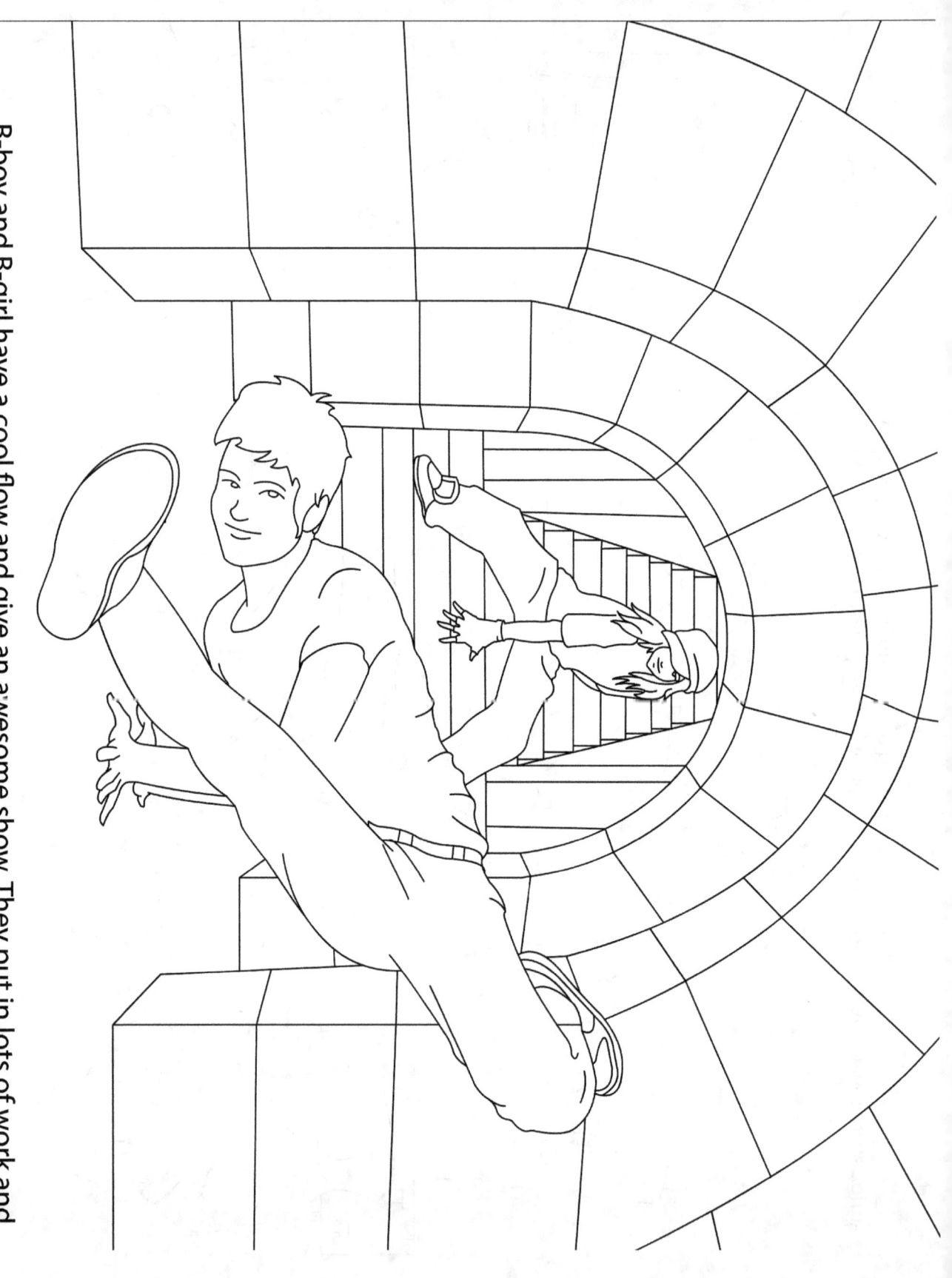

B-boy and B-girl have a cool flow and give an awesome show. They put in lots of work and time so their breakdance moves are sublime.

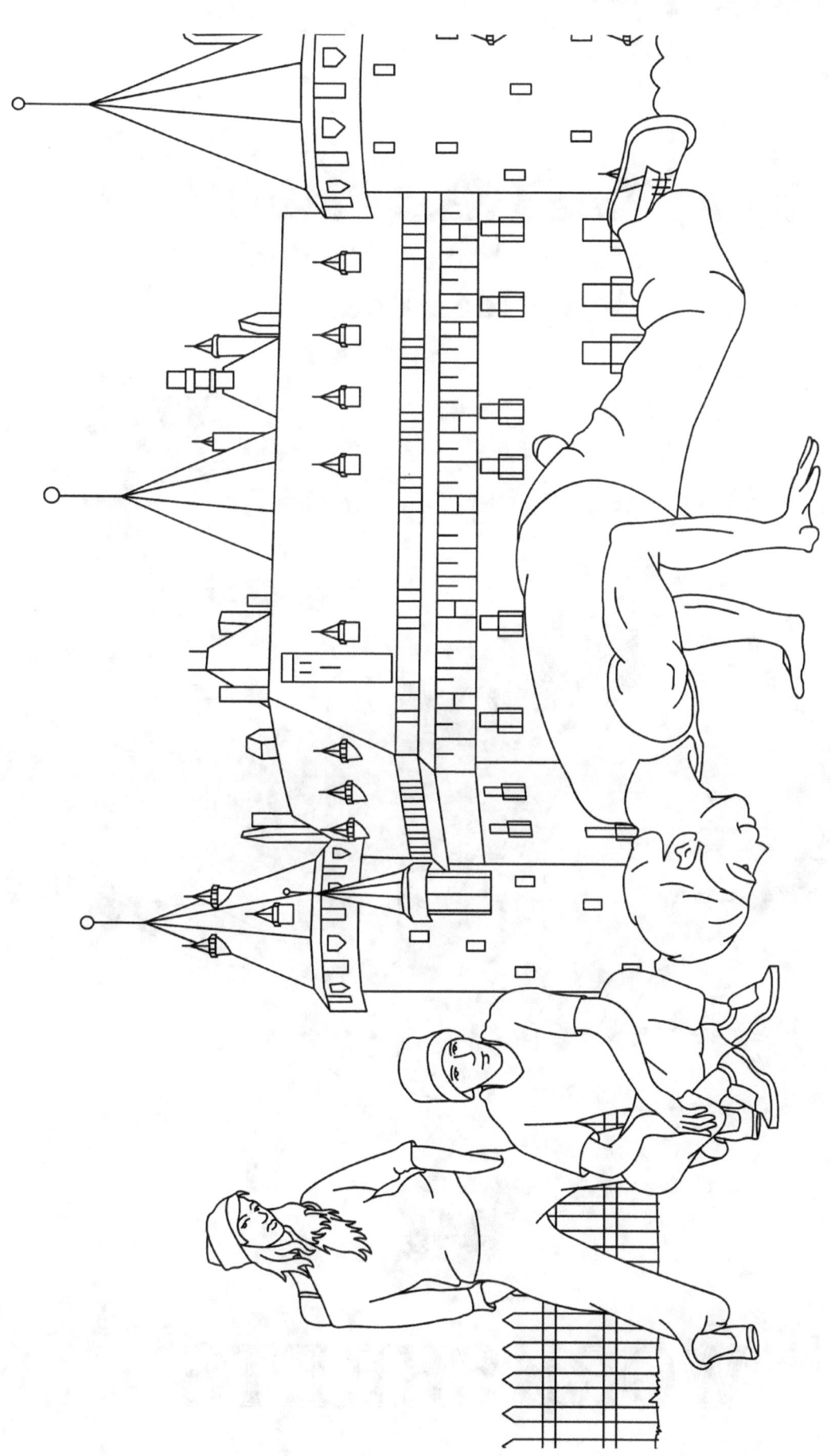

Get ready for the next body-ride, here he comes with the hand-glide. With hands in a strong position, he glides swift without collision. Breakdancing takes all parts of your body to pull off moves that are Godly.

BREAKDANCE

Coloring & Activity Book
by Idan Boaz

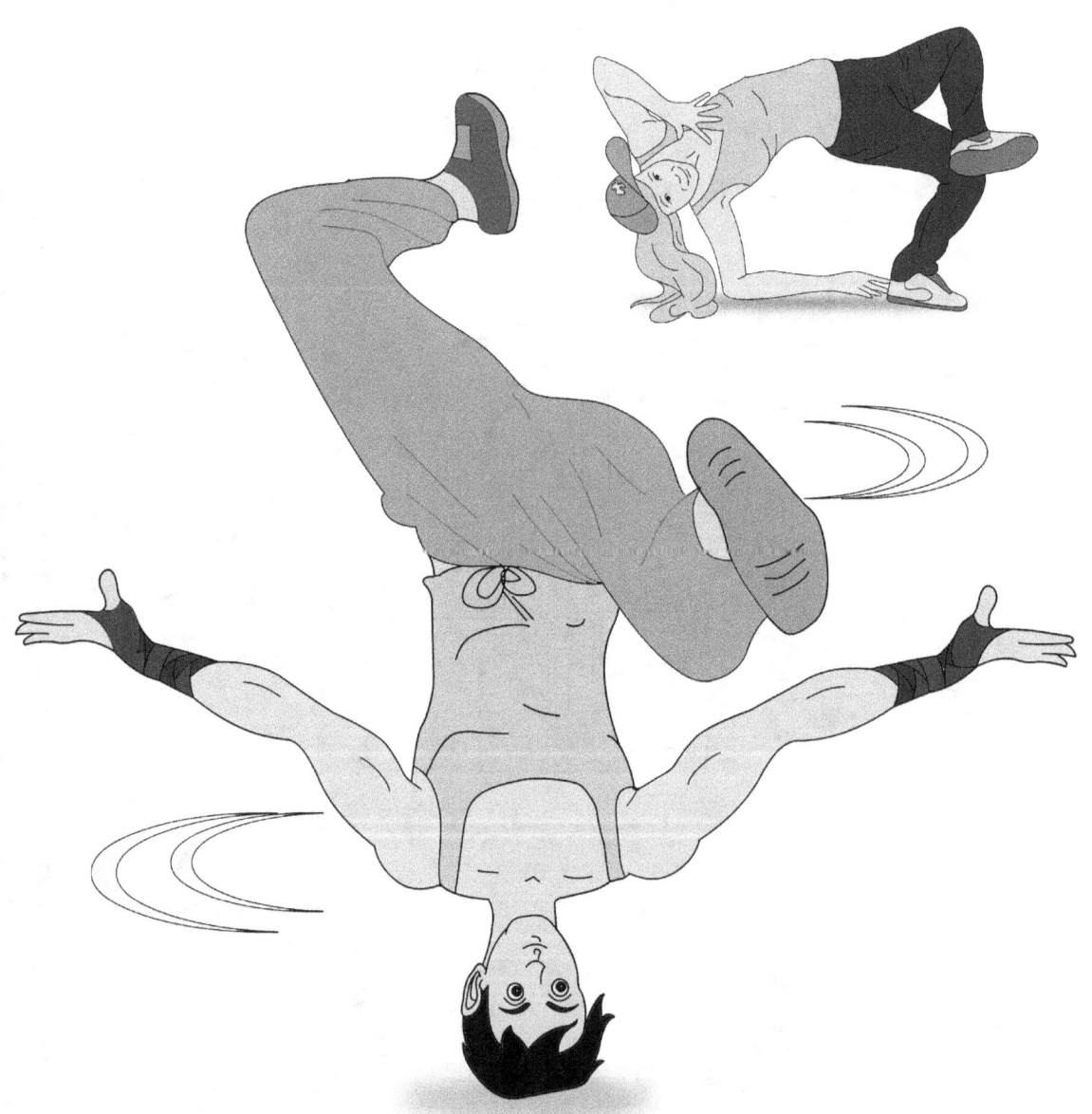

WORKSHEETS

Please help the DJ get his wire into the amp

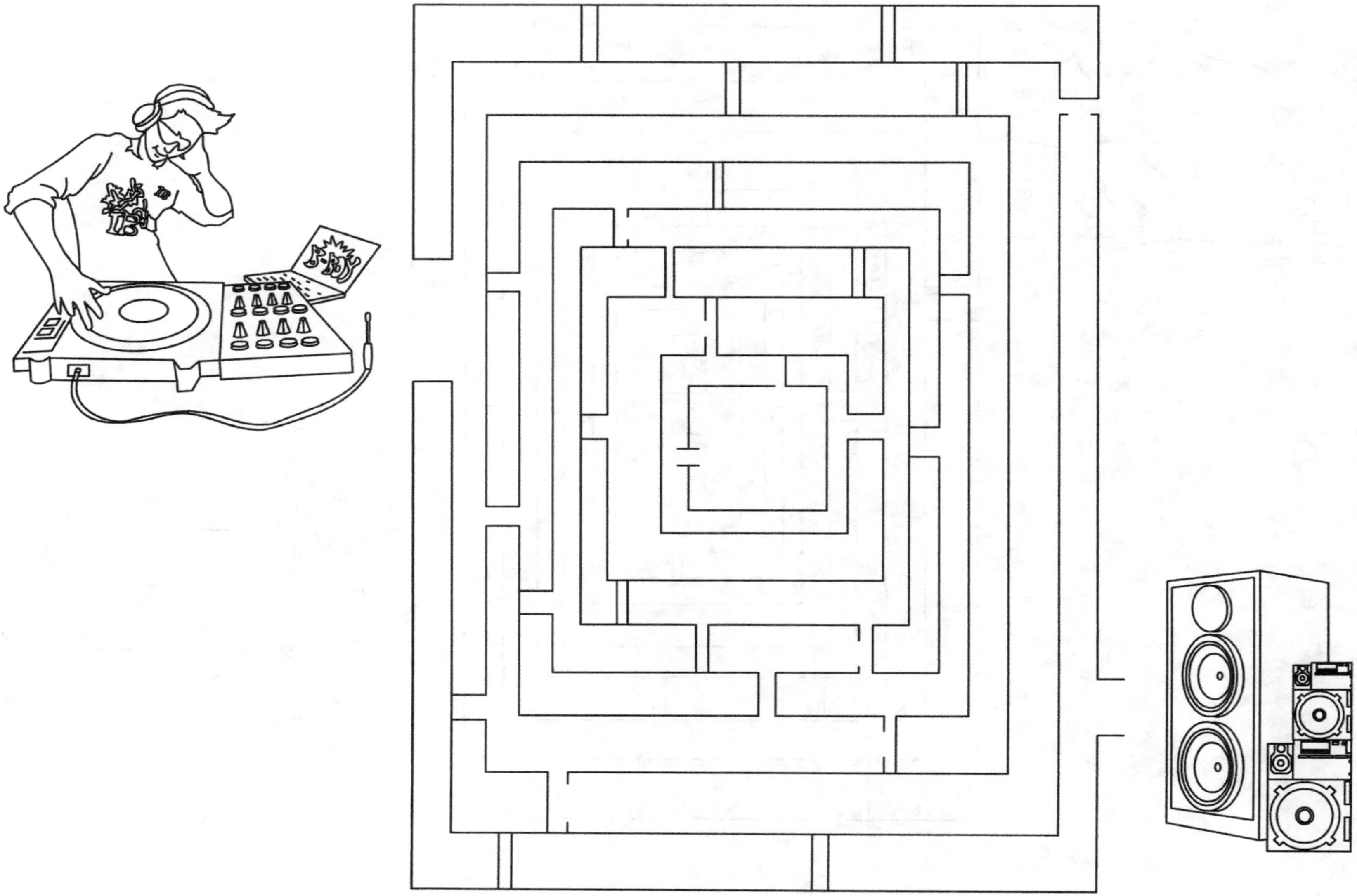

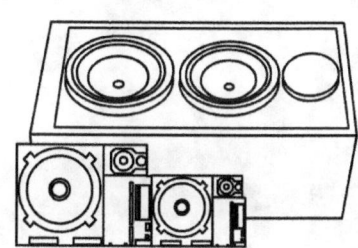

Please help the B-Girl get to the photo shoot

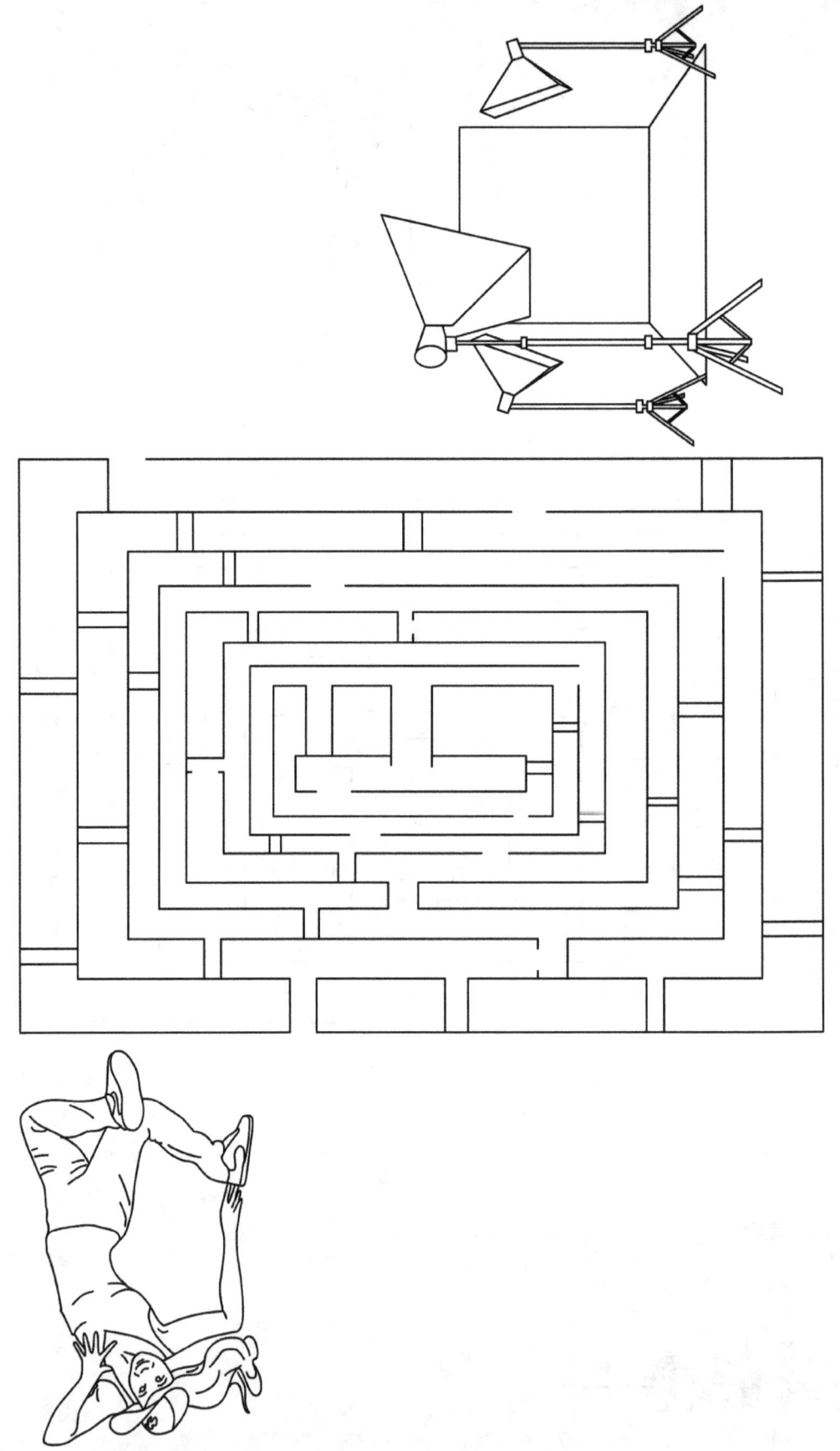

Spot 4 Differences

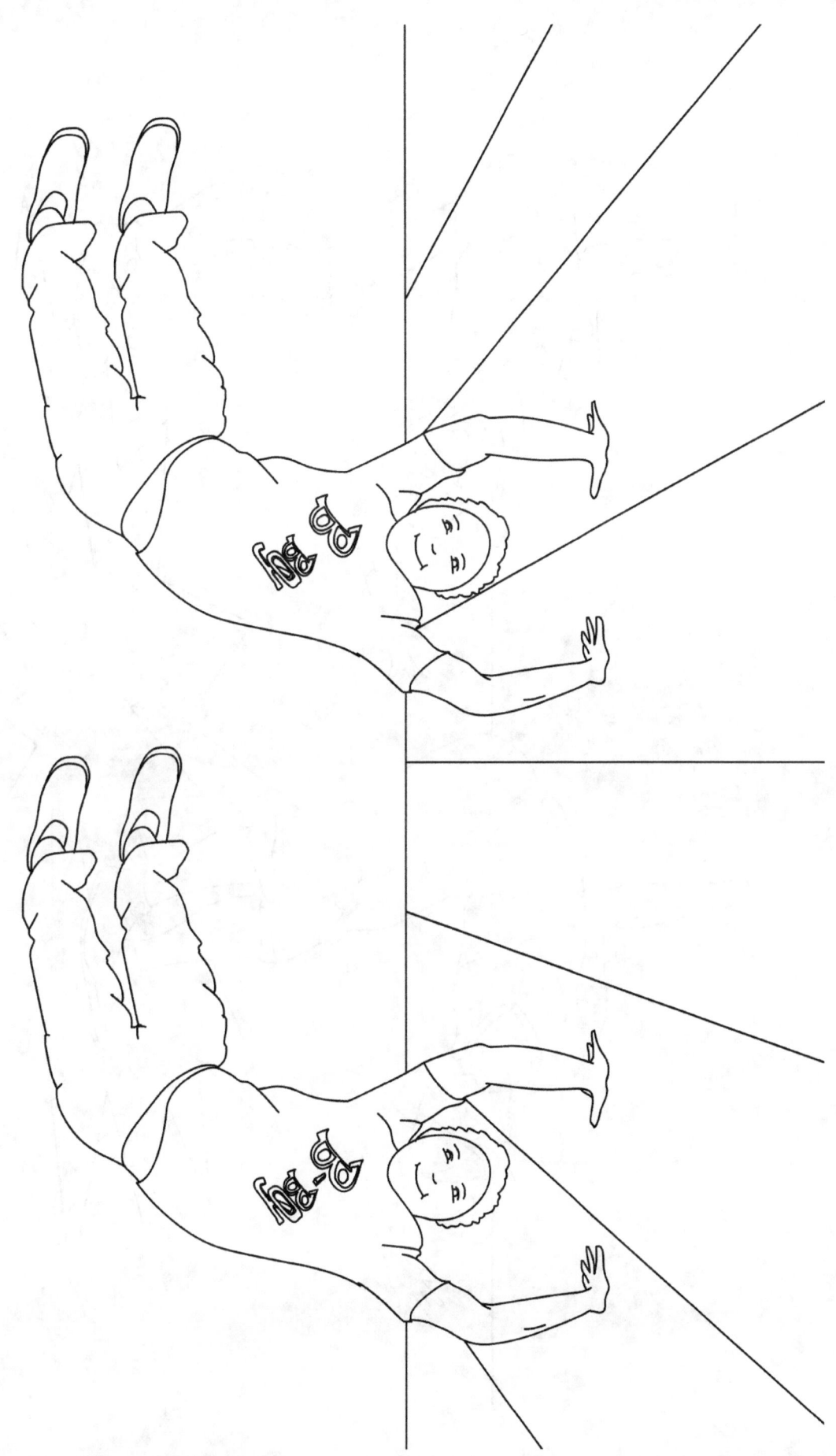

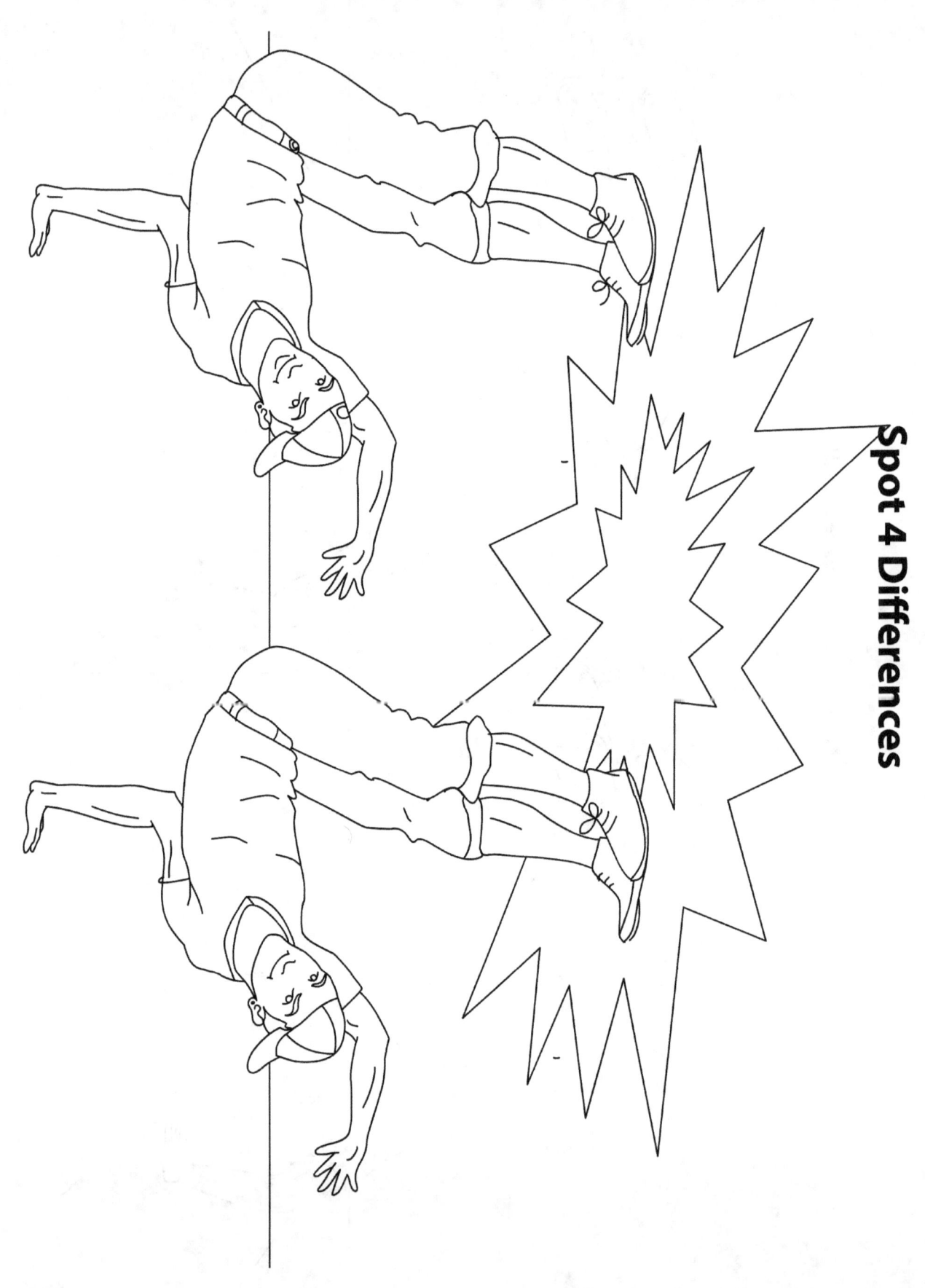

Spot 4 Differences

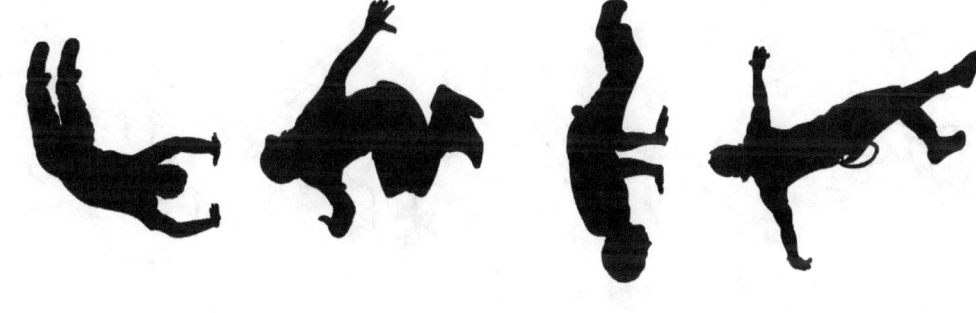

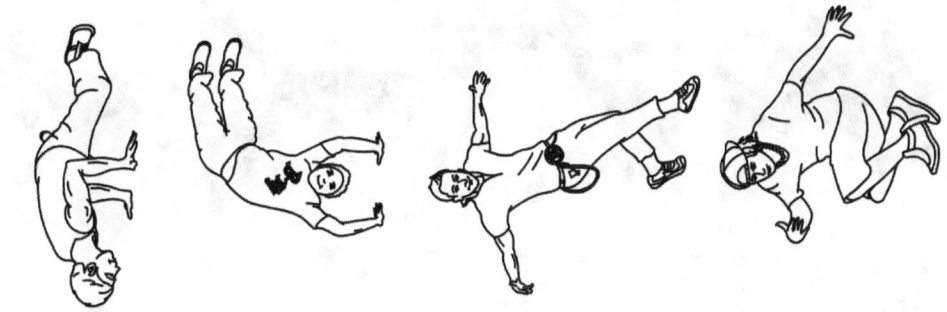

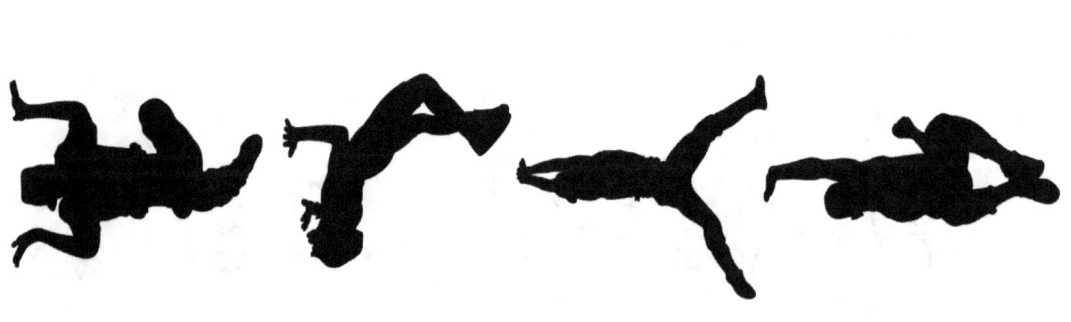

Copy the Dancer

Copy the picture using the grid lines as a guide.
You might find it easier to copy one square at a time.

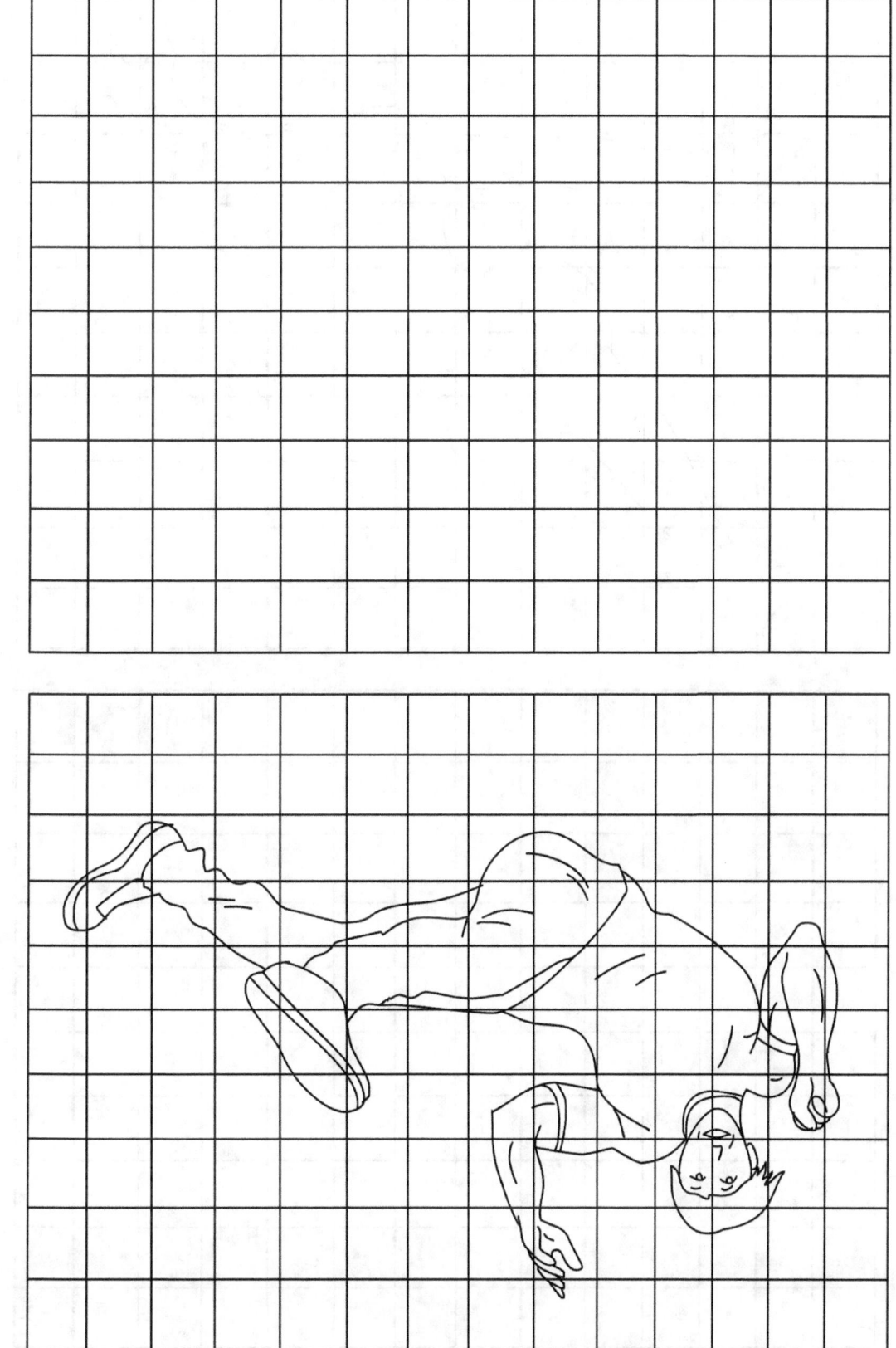

Copy the Dancer

Copy the picture using the grid lines as a guide.
You might find it easier to copy one square at a time.

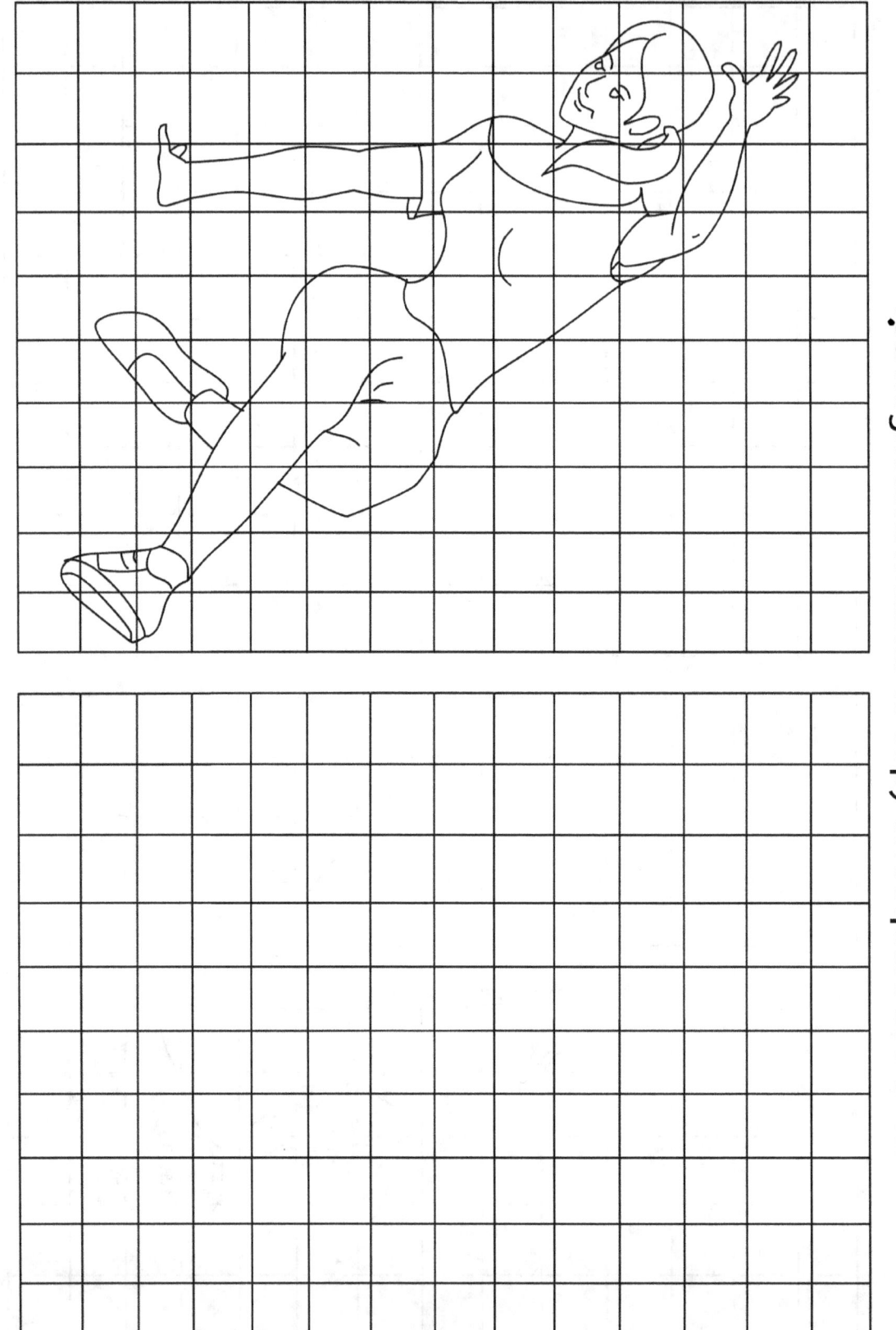

Cut Out & Play

1. Color and cut out all the parts.
2. Arrange parts by order.

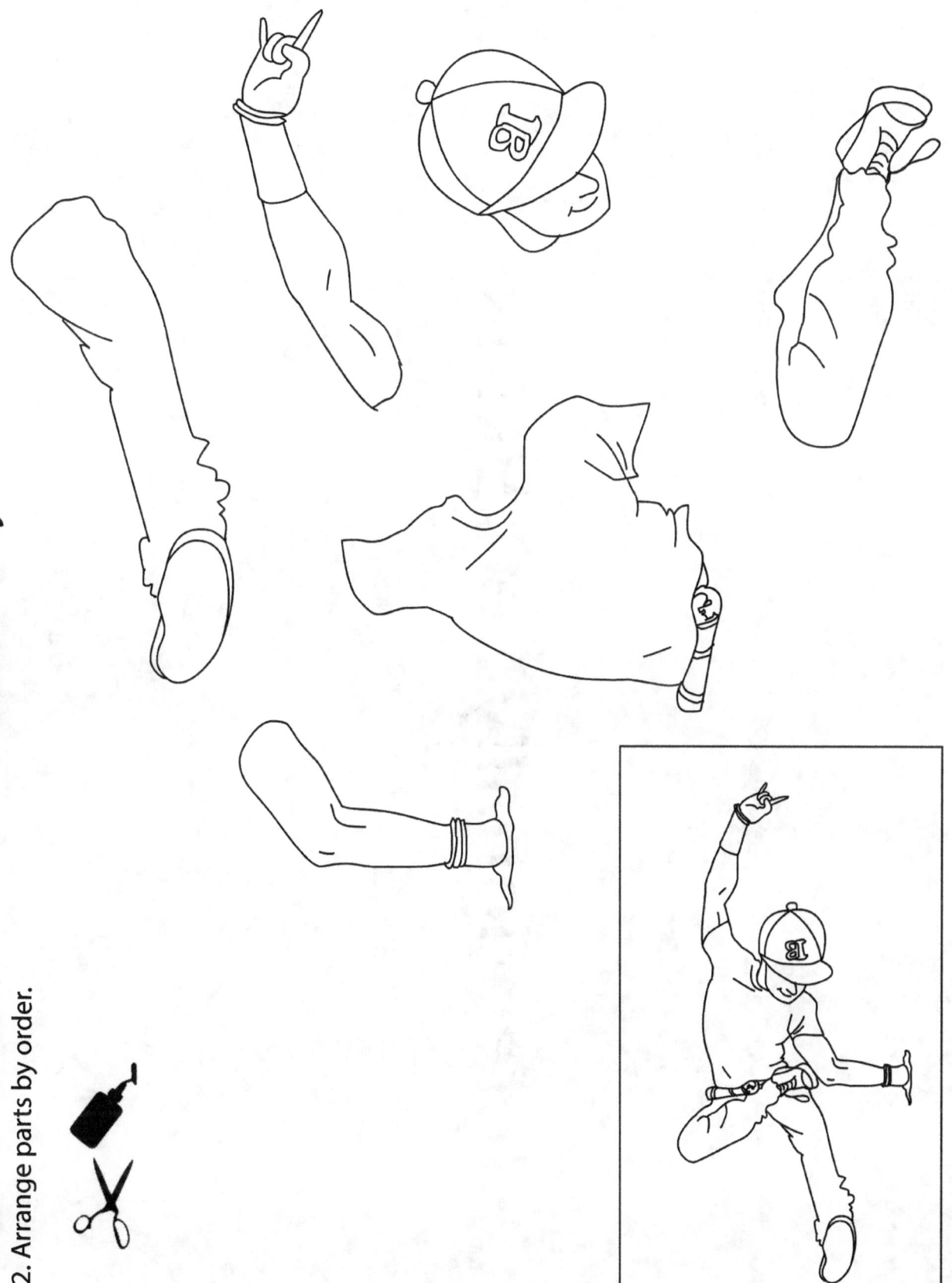

Intentionally Left Blank

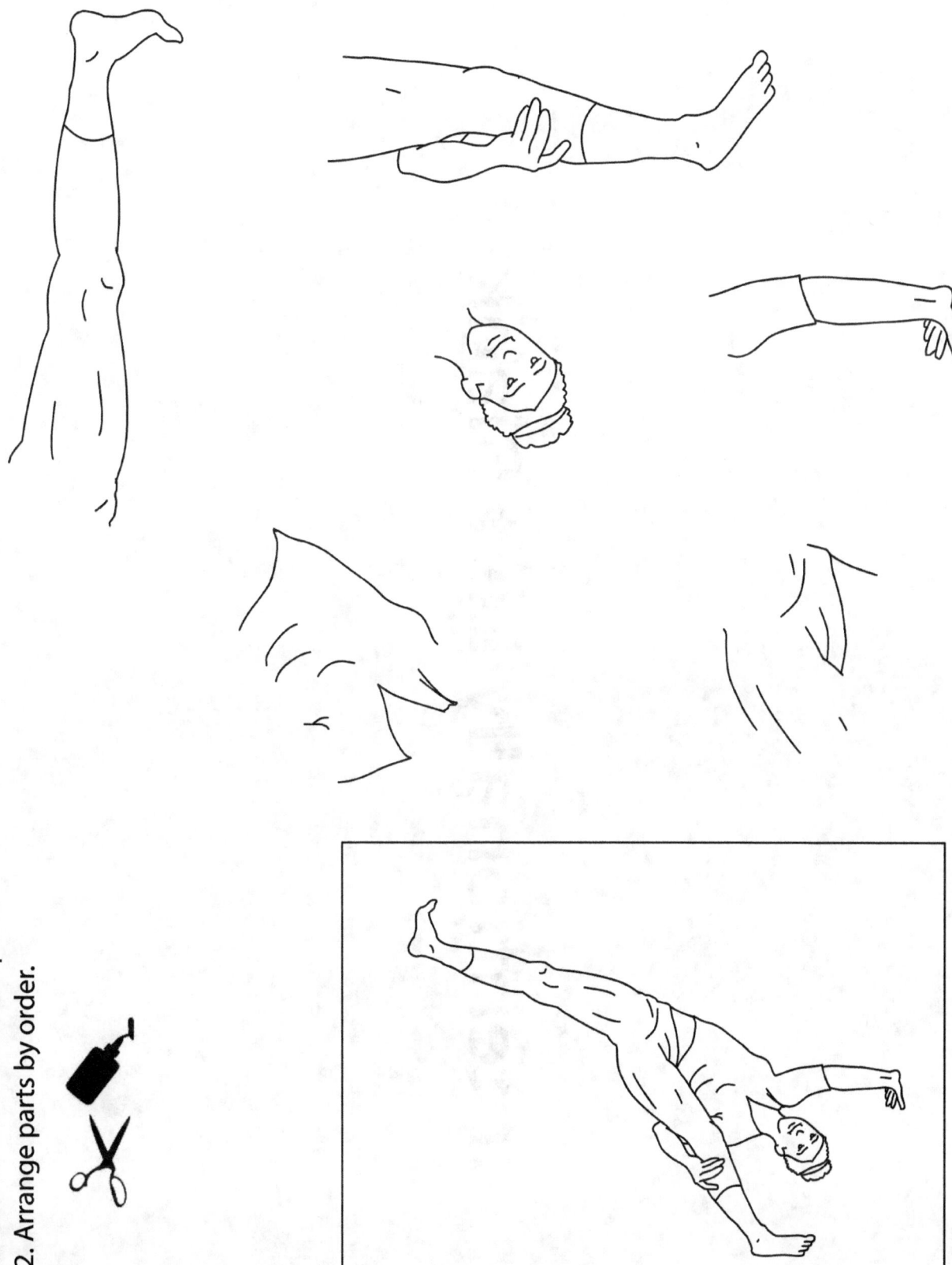

Cut Out & Play

1. Color and cut out all the parts.
2. Arrange parts by order.

Intentionally Left Blank

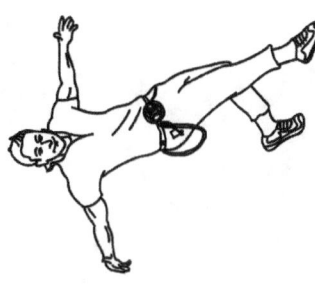
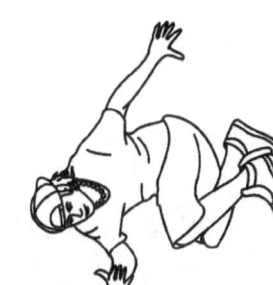
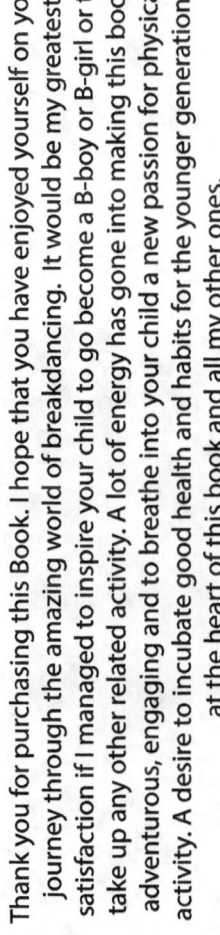
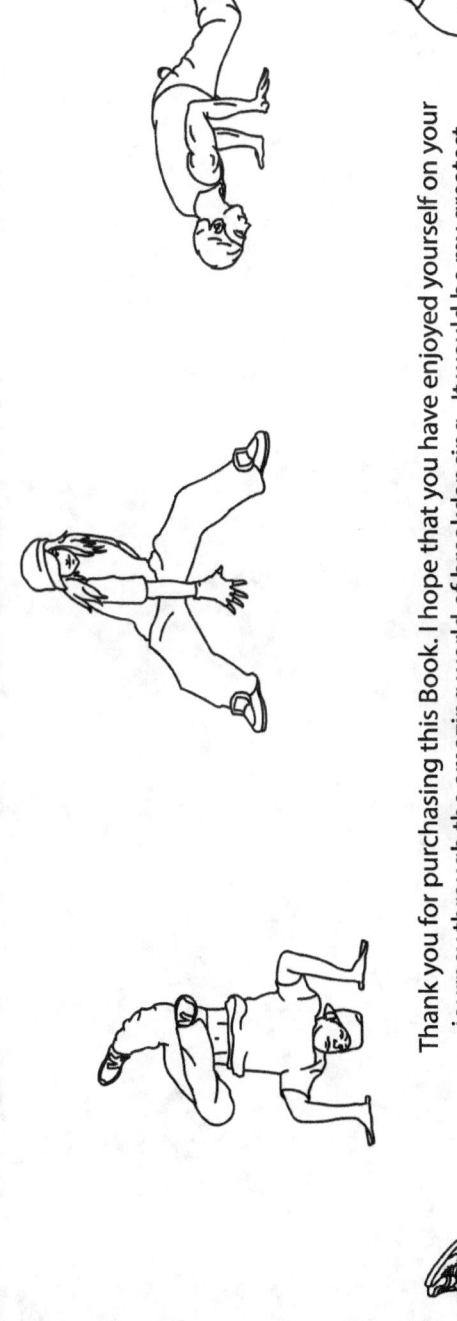
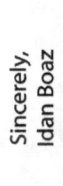
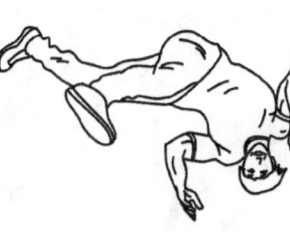

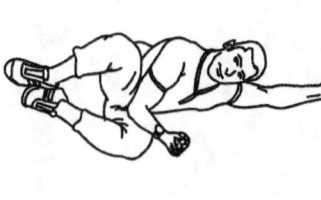

Thank you for purchasing this Book. I hope that you have enjoyed yourself on your journey through the amazing world of breakdancing. It would be my greatest satisfaction if I managed to inspire your child to go become a B-boy or B-girl or to take up any other related activity. A lot of energy has gone into making this book adventurous, engaging and to breathe into your child a new passion for physical activity. A desire to incubate good health and habits for the younger generation is at the heart of this book and all my other ones.

Therefore I ask if there is any way I can make my books even more engaging, or if there is something you enjoyed, would like to see more of and help spread the word to others, please go to Amazon to leave a review. And, if you really enjoyed this book, you can find all my other books on my Amazon page.

Sincerely,
Idan Boaz
If you have any comments or advice, please write me:
info@idanboaz.co.il
www.author.idanboaz.co.il
www.ib-books.com

www.ingramcontent.com/pod-product-compliance
Lightning Source LLC
Chambersburg PA
CBHW081821170526
45167CB00008B/3489

* 9 7 8 1 5 4 4 0 9 1 2 5 9 *